Andretti

Text by Mario Andretti

Foreword by Paul Newman

Edited by Mark Vancil

CollinsPublishersSanFrancisco

A Division of HarperCollins*Publishers*

Produced by:
Rare Air, Ltd.
A Mark Vancil Company

Designed by:
John Vieceli

McMillan Associates
130 Washington
West Dundee, IL 60118

Special Thanks to:
Michael McMillan, Anne McMillan, Laura Vancil, Jane Haka,
Paul Sheridan, Walter Iooss Jr., Jim Forni, Jim O'Donnell,
John Balla and Amy Hollowbush.

At Sports Management Network:
John Caponigro, Mike McEvoy, Rena Shanaman, and
John Schram.

First published 1994 by Collins Publishers San Francisco

Andretti. Copyright © 1994 Rare Air, Ltd.

Text © Mario Andretti

Photographs©:
Walter Iooss Jr. Cover, 10, 28, 29, 30, 48-49, 51, 54-55, 56, 58,
59, 60, 61, 62, 63, 65, 66, 69, 70, 72, 73, 74, 75, 76, 84-85, 93,
96, 97, 109, 113, 114; Andretti family 1, 12, 35, 52, 64, 68, 99;
Dan Boyd 46-47, 96; Bruce Craig 7, 15, 16, 17, 18, 20-21, 32, 38,
39, 40-41, 82, 86, 87, 92, 100, 101, 106, 107; Joe DiMaggio 42-43;
Dave Friedman 22, 23, 78, 87, 88, 89, 90-91, 104, 105, 106, 107;
Jutta Fausel 103; Don Hodgdon 80-81; Ron Hoskins 57, 68;
Indianapolis Speedway 16, 36, 37, 44, back page; Raymond Masser
16, 17; Michael McMillan 67, 94; Sandro Miller 4, 8-9, 56, 57, 110-
111; Sports Illustrated 108; George Tiedemann 24-25, 26, 83, 89,
107; ThierryThompson 2-3, 102.

Collins Publishers San Francisco books may be purchased for
educational, business, or sales promotion use. For information,
please call or write: Special Markets Department, Collins Publishers
San Francisco, 1160 Battery Street, San Francisco, California 94111.
Telephone: (415) 788-4111.

First Edition
Library of Congress Cataloging-in-Publication Data
Andretti, Mario, 1940–.
Andretti/Text by Mario Andretti; Edited by Mark Vancil.
p. cm.
ISBN 0-00-255486-0—ISBN 0-00-638302-5 (pbk.)

1. Andretti, Mario, 1940–. 2. Automobile racing driver—United
States—Biography. 3. Andretti, Mario, 1940–. Pictorial works.
I. Vancil, Mark, 1958–. II. Title.
GV1032.A5A3 1994

796.7'2'092—dc20   94-30162
[B]   CIP

Printed in the United States of America
10 9 8 7 6 5 4 3 2 1

For Dee Ann.

From the bright light of victory to the dark shadow of defeat, you have been by my side.

Whether in person or in spirit, I knew you were with me every time I stepped into a race car.

I couldn't have made it to the end without you.

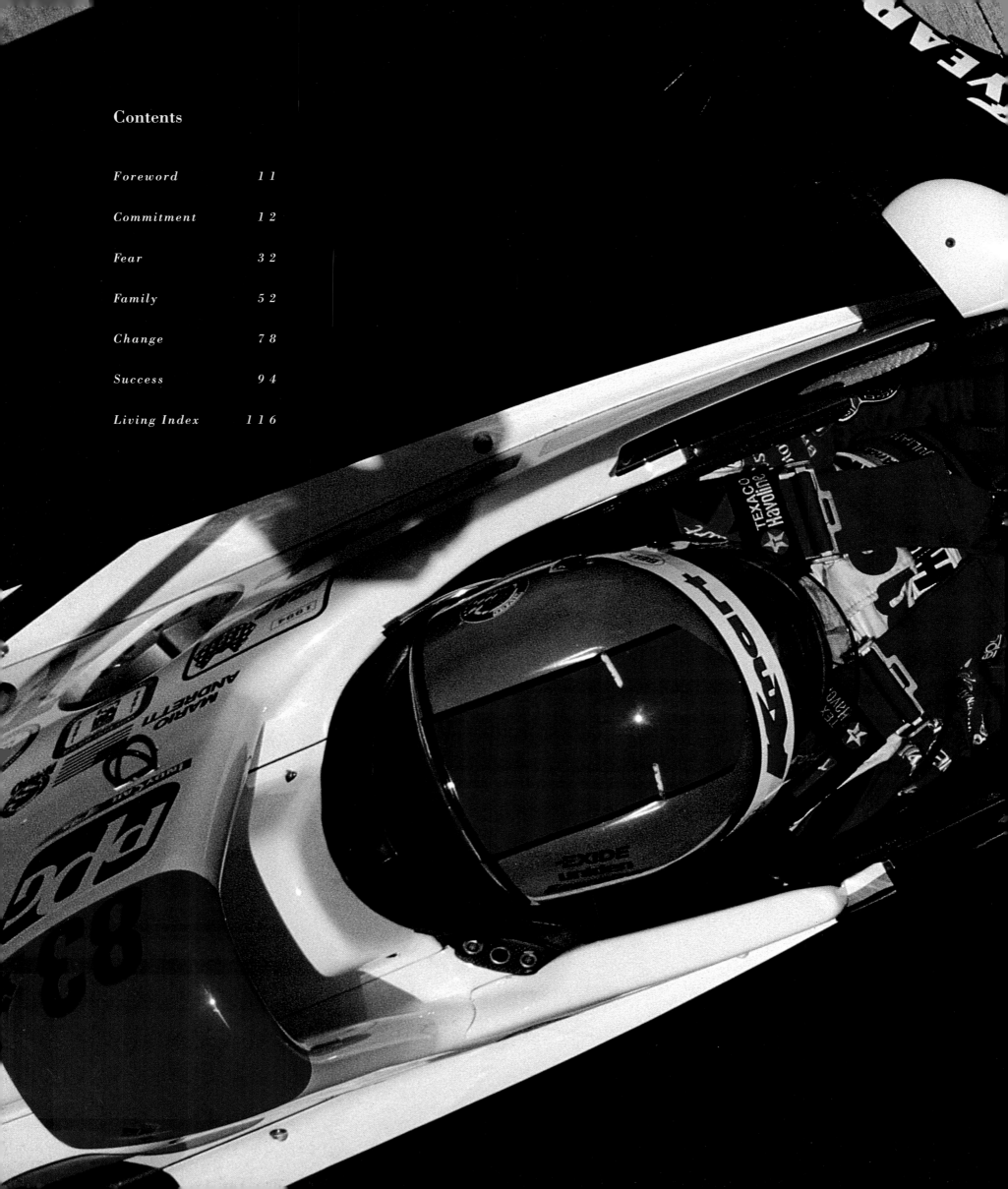

Contents

Foreword

by Paul Newman

Everyone knows the legend that is Mario Andretti. It's in the record books.

It is also audible in the applause at Drivers Introductions. Louder and more boisterous for Mario than anyone.

It's on a handmade t-shirt at Indy:

"*Everyone sucks, except Mario.*"

On a sheet draped over a camper at Michigan:

"*Blessed are the Marios*

For they shall inherit the Earth."

I wonder how much I can add to so much that is known.

Well...

It is not necessarily known that, next to family, friends, the Church, and the combustion engine, Mario Andretti is devoted to his pig, Martini.

On a Sunday afternoon at Andretti Lake not long ago, I watched the two of them as they bonded together on the lawn.

The family looked on in dismay.

I clear my throat to get his attention.

"What in God's name is the allure of that pig?" I ask.

"The allure of the pig is considerable and it is obvious. The pig is very much his own man. Not like dogs. He does not maneuver or have a secret agenda. He has no angle to play and is not on the chisel. Look at him! There is absolutely nothing between you and the pig. The pig is incorruptible."

I remember my first notes when I started to write this introduction.

"Mario is incorruptible. He is his own man and has no secret agenda. He is not on the chisel..."

I shift my weight nervously from foot to foot. One is, as you can well imagine, cautious of, well. . . I mean, if a comparison. . .

Thin ice is everywhere.

Now that I think on it, at our very first meeting in 1967, there was a pig involved.

A chassis.

Built by an extremely gifted designer who had called me.

"You ever heard of Mario Andretti?"

"Is the Pope Catholic?"

"How about we put your name on Mario Andretti's Cam Am car?"

"You betcha! Nifty!" says I.

Well, we got off to a bad start. Nothing about this particular vehicle worked. It was nervous, changed direction badly, pushed, rolled and chattered.

He brought the car in from qualifying, spat, shook my hand, and studied the car.

The first words from Mario Andretti to Paul Newman were: "How about I put my name on it and you try to drive?"

So much for guile.

By way of getting even, he took me around Bridgehampton in a 427 ci. Mustang...my first ride with a professional driver. As we approached a fourth gear, blind, downhill right-hander, I thought I'd have a better chance of surviving Custer's Last Stand than this.

When we stopped in the pits, I hurled myself from the infernal machine, belly down, kissed the ground, thanked my Maker, and vowed never again to kick my dog, or, as it turned out later, his pig.

It (the pig) surfaced again in 1983 when Mario, Carl Haas, and I started Newman/Haas Racing. The first Lola we gave him rooted out tire walls the length and breadth of every track from coast to coast. We made up for it in 1984 and gave Mario a car with which he won the title.

And then, there are lulls in our conversation. Mario is, for all his conviviality, a very private person. I am a very private person. Once we exhaust sway bars and seafood, there are silences of consequence. We used to discuss politics when we first met and were middle-of-the-roaders. Now, Mario has ascended to a kind of Free-Wheeling Conservative Gorilla Individualism while I moved crabwise toward a Middle-of-the-Road Fundamental Anarchist. Like I said, we used to discuss politics, but we wore each other out.

Arie Luyendyk and I watch Mario clamber out of the car this year at Toronto. After a very long, very hot, teeth-rattling race, the bala-clava gets thrown into his helmet.

"Look at him," says Arie. "His Goddamn hair ain't even wet."

Yeah. Drives you nuts, don't it?

We went to the opera a few years ago, the Andrettis and the Newmans. We supped in the plush dining room at Lincoln Center. I was somewhat astonished to watch the normally aloof maitre d' thundering toward us, scattering patrons and waiters like bowling pins in his effort to get to our table then transformed himself into Uriah Heep.

"Mr. Andretti. Oh, my. Champagne?"

"As you like," replied Mario.

"Dom Perignon or Crystal? It's on the house."

I steamed. Joanne and I had been coming to this self-same eatery for twenty years without so much as a hint of free Budweiser.

"Are you Italian, or something?" I asked crankily.

"From Rhodesia," he replied.

It figures.

Mario's esteem covers the globe like a blanket.

They always used to say, 'Man, if the kid survives, he'll be good.' I used to hear that all the time. Jim McGee used to send me Christmas cards in July because he didn't think I was going to make it to December. That was music to my ears because I knew what they thought: 'At least he stands on the button, so as soon as he learns how to do it right, he'll really go.' You have to show that burning desire. When you show that, nobody faults you. That's what I've found.

Alberto Ascari was cool. That's what I used to love about him. He was described as having ice-cold blood. When I saw photographs of him in action, I could see he had a certain flair. He was quick, yes, but he was cool. And he was doing it with control and a style that was all his own. It was really appealing to a young kid.

I first became interested in motor racing when I was probably 11 or 12. You have to understand, in those days, motor racing was more popular than any other sport in Italy.

That was especially true in the 1950s, when you had Ferrari, Maserati, and Alfa Romeo. They were the standards for racing around the world. Also, the first world champion was an Italian, Nino Farina. And the world champion when I was growing up in the early 1950s was Alberto Ascari. He became my idol.

In Italy, all that my twin brother, Aldo, and I had was the radio and the newsreels we'd see at the movies. There was no television. In fact, I used to go to movies just to see the newsreels because that was the only time you could see racing in action.

We were sophisticated enough to know the schedule and I used to buy the racing magazines every week. So I was pretty much up on what was happening. In those days there were not as many races, but the coverage was there. And I was always looking forward to the next race.

But it all hadn't sunk in yet. I knew there was something going on out there. There were guys doing it and I knew I wanted to be one of them.

Just the looks of the cars, the drivers, and their gear, all of that fascinated me. For me, it all started with the goggles, the kind I wore when I first started racing. They were just like the ones Ascari wore.

He was the best, no question. He was winning, and that's really what attracted me to him. There were other guys I loved to watch race, but they were not my role models. They might have been doing well, but my role model was the guy doing the winning. For some people, winning is all they'll accept. It becomes ingrained in them. I see a lot of that in my son Michael. And it was that way with me.

You look at my record over the years, and I've had a lot of races where either I won or I was right there. But if I didn't win, it didn't mean a thing. Second and third didn't matter to me. Which is not always the best way to look at things. I don't always condone that kind of thinking. Sometimes you can be a little smarter, a little more patient, and still be satisfied. You develop that with maturity, an element that ultimately works in your favor.

But in the beginning, man, I had to win. I *had* to win. Sometimes that desire cost me by spinning or getting into crashes. At the same time, looking at the whole picture and what that aggression delivered for me, what it got me over the years, I think if I had approached racing any other way, I probably wouldn't have succeeded.

In my case, I couldn't have it all. I couldn't be patient and, at the same time, maintain my aggression. I had to be one or the other. As I said, it's not the best quality. Sometimes I wish I would have come to that realization sooner. But again, that was my style, and that's what I had to live with.

It's hard to assess whether there is much of Ascari in me. But I hope the best in me is what Ascari had in him.

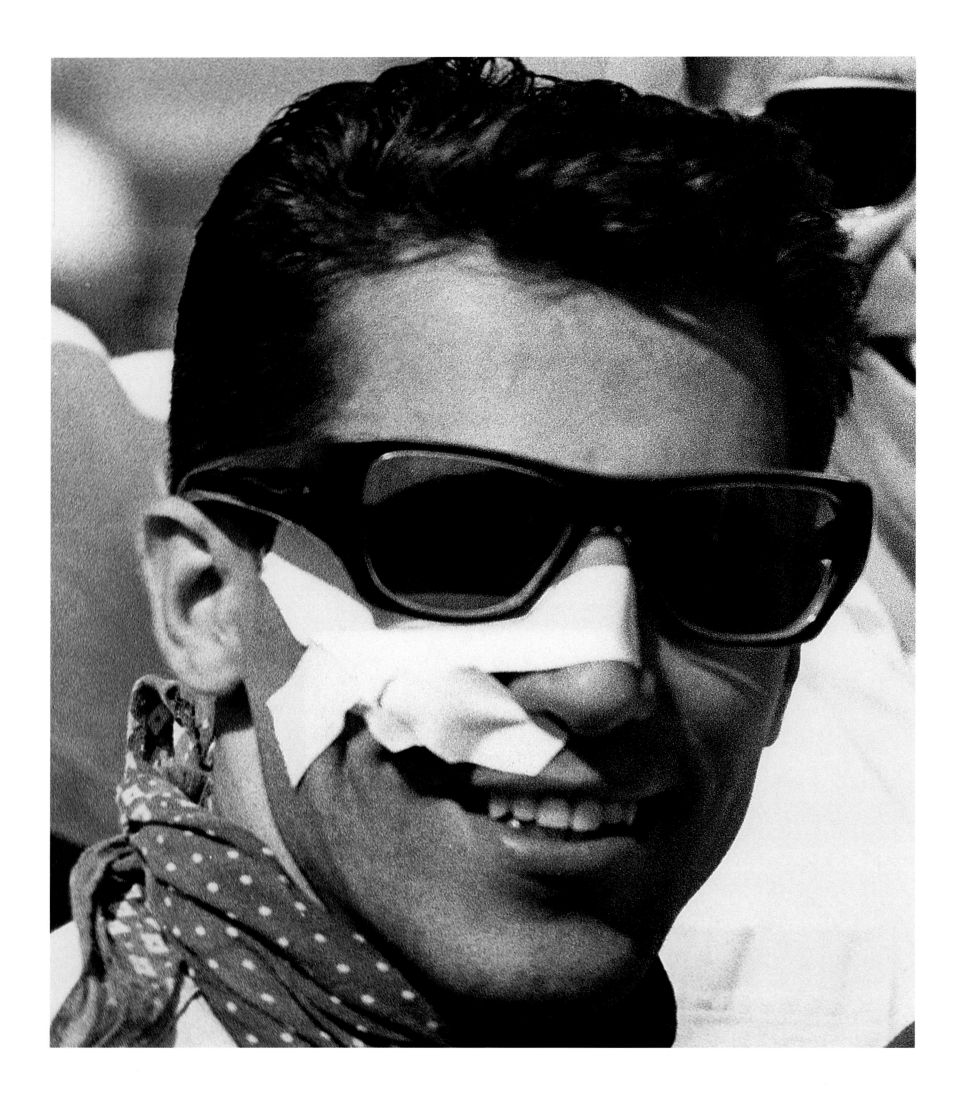

I've been lucky. In all my days of racing, I've never missed an event because of illness. And I've only been forced out of two races because of an injury.

After crashing in the Michigan 500 in 1985, I missed the next race at Elkhart Lake. I ended up with a cracked pelvis, three broken ribs, and a broken clavicle. By the time we got to Pocono, the pelvis and everything else had not totally healed.

Don't forget, the race was on Sunday, but we started practicing on Thursday. So it had been only two and a half weeks since the accident. And Pocono was going to be tough because the track was so bumpy. But I refused to sit out another race.

So I contacted a company in Texas called Spanco that specialized in energy-absorbing products. They gave us all kinds of options to pad the cockpit. Unfortunately, the material wasn't firm enough. So even though it was protecting all of my injuries, I had no feel for the car. As a result, we had to throw away about 50 percent of the padding.

Without that product, I couldn't have made it. Even then, however, it was tough. I remember this old-timer came over, slapped me on the shoulder, and said, 'Hey man, how are you doing?' I saw stars.

The point is, I finished the race. And I have done that several times in pain. I've raced with broken ribs, and that's the worst pain there is. I can assure you, it was never any fun, but that's the price you have to pay if you're going to compete at the highest level.

I found from day one, even with the first car Aldo and I owned, you could do certain things to the car to help yourself. Through the years I have found that being willing and able to investigate and understand what makes the car work pays off in the end. For me that was a natural process. It came to me instinctively and I put that information to maximum use.

But it goes with the territory if you're going to succeed. You have to find all the advantages possible. If you're in business, you want to be sharper than the guy down the road. You want to advertise better, create a better product to sell.

That's why everything in racing parallels real life in so many ways. It's about improving yourself, finding the edge that makes you just a little quicker out on the track. All this takes time and it can be tedious, even frustrating. But it all goes toward that ultimate reward.

There are guys that win a race once in a while. But then there are the guys that win races consistently. And you can count those on the fingers of one hand. You can look at Formula One, NASCAR, or Indy Cars, and it's always the same.

There are very few drivers that know how to win. They work extremely hard and they don't relax because it's too easy to relax.

It's ability, but it's also desire. You see, a lot of people are content to just be there. I watched my good friend, coach Dick Vermeil, and I knew Philadelphia wouldn't win the Super Bowl in 1981. Why? Because they were just happy being there. I was on my way down to Miami to connect with a flight to Buenos Aires so I couldn't watch the game. But I saw the National Anthem, and I could tell, looking into their eyes, they weren't going to win. Then you saw Oakland, and those guys were ready. Philadelphia looked like a bunch of altar boys, and I thought, 'They're going to get killed.'

That's the difference between winning and just being happy to be there. There are a lot of guys that have been on the podium but have never won. You hear about them all the time. This guy or that guy had so many top 10 finishes. And they're happy. But they run hundreds of races and never win because they don't understand the ingredient.

It's talent and instinct, but it's also that desire, that pride that comes with accomplishment. I remember watching Michael. The first go-cart race I ever put him in, that kid knew he had to get up front. He didn't know how, but all he had in mind was to run over guys, bang into them, whatever. Now that's scary in a go-cart.

I thought, this kid is going to win every race he can. If he finishes second, it will be because it's impossible to win that race. It was that kind of a deal. I mean, he had it going and he was only nine.

But this is not something that grows into your character. You are either born with that desire and instinct or you're not. You aren't born with a steering wheel in your hand or anything like that.

I believe it's inside somehow. Character cannot be taught, just as you cannot teach intensity. You can tell somebody they need to be intense, but unless they truly understand, it won't happen. If a guy has to try to understand or if he has to be forced to learn, then he's not going to be consistent. Why? Because it's unnatural.

But every element of success requires work. If it's something you want, then you have to go out and work at it. That's why the average guy is laid back. Hell, that's easy. It's convenient to be mediocre.

It's the intensity, the desire, that develops the talent. If you watch somebody else and he's going faster, you have to ask yourself why. You know you have to work on something.

I've always had that intensity. Actually I was overzealous when I was young. I had all this energy, and I didn't know how to distribute it. As a result, I had a tendency to overdo things. How much better off would I have been if I had only known how to distribute that energy properly? Have I lost races because of my overzealousness? Damned right I have.

That's one thing I tried to teach my kids early. Don't be overly aggressive. Hold back. But it's much easier said than done. Still, that's one reason I've always thought that race to race, Michael was light-years ahead of me for his age in terms of maturity and what he knew versus what I knew at the same time in my career.

In the '70s, I was driving everything I could get my hands on. I was going from one extreme to another, from Formula One to running dirt in DuQuoin.

I used to do that week in and week out. To me, it was not only challenging but also fascinating. And the opportunities were there. One weekend I might run a stock car on a road course at Mosport, and the next I'd run on dirt at the Indianapolis Fairgrounds.

But simply competing in those events was not the point. Competing and winning is what was important. I mean, it's like I've got my own little playground here and I know where all the tunnels are. So when you come over, I can beat you at whatever game we play because I have the advantage.

When I go into your playground, you know all the tricks, so I'm supposed to feel a little out of place. But if I can outdo you on your playground, then it's like, man, what the hell does this guy have? That was the whole idea.

And that's the game I played with myself. That's why it was a fascinating challenge. I needed a lot of luck along the way, no question. But, man, I had to be there.

And those are the memories I will always cherish because that kind of opportunity isn't there for today's drivers. The commitments are so tight that you almost have to specialize. I don't mean just the driving itself, but the contractual obligations as well.

You get into a contract today and raise the issue of being free to do this or that, and it becomes a huge issue. Take Michael, for example. He wanted to do some sports prototypes. Suddenly there are insurance questions regarding the contract, and next thing you know, there are another 18 pages of legal details.

When I was his age, if somebody said they weren't going to let me do something, I'd be ready to punch them. You mean you're going to tell me what to do? You want me to drive? I'll drive. But after that, I'll do what I want. If I want to drive motorcycles, I'll do it.

I had a rather arrogant approach in that no one was going to dictate to me. I've kept that issue of freedom to this day as part of all my negotiations. They don't even challenge it anymore.

I prepare for every race exactly the same, no longer, no shorter.

I get up, depending upon what's going on that morning, and try to give myself the same amount of time before each event. If I can sleep another half hour, I will. As a matter of fact, when I'm under pressure, I have this sense or ability to relax even more.

I like to be left alone and stay clear of any small talk in the hours before a race. I just want to be in my own place, profiling the race in my mind. I think about the start, how the car will be running. I'm trying to figure out the nuances of that particular track, the stops, where they will be, what the landmarks are so that I don't overshoot the pit area. Once I'm in the car, I try to visualize all the things that are going to be a part of the race, all the things I know I will be experiencing, everything I should be aware of. Because of that process, I sometimes try to go aside, by myself, away from everyone.

But many of these same thoughts are with me every day in one form or another. When I say I'm working 24 hours a day, that means I can be in the middle of a meal or sipping a glass of wine and boom, something hits me. We've got to try that. You have to keep your mind fertile and open at all times if you want to stay on top.

But you also must have the ability to keep your mind focused. If racing is your main business, then that's got to be No. 1, *numero uno*. It comes down to some very simple questions. How much time are you willing to be thinking about your business? Is it troublesome to always have your mind on work? Would you rather be thinking about other things, such as golfing, boating, and that sort of thing?

If you want to compete at the highest levels, then everything else has to slide to the side. That's the way I've always felt. Nothing will interfere with my work. Nothing will *ever* interfere with my work. If I fail, I know I will have given it my all.

This focus is important at every level of life, really. That's why, ultimately, I've always thought limits are really defined only by your imagination.

You learn as much as you can about a race car, more than the mere mechanics and setup. You must develop that feel so that it becomes a part of your senses.

That's when you begin to know how to take a car to the limit without going beyond. That's the trick.

In that sense, a car is like an animal. You can push and push until you do something that makes that animal start biting. But how do you know where that point is? The great search is to go as close as possible without falling over. To win, you have to ride right on the edge. That's where champions are made. And that's the difference between the great drivers and all the others.

I don't know what it is, but I know it's something that comes with time. And in the end, the only thing that matters is winning. It drowns out everything else. That's the payoff. And for me, the reward always justified the risk.

If I had stopped
and really reflected on
the danger just once, I
probably never would have
stepped back in a race car. As
realistic as you wanted to be,
you almost didn't want to think about it. I was
driven by something different. I was driven by
the desire to race at all costs. But I didn't want to
know what the costs were. Otherwise, there is no
way in my own mind that I could have rationalized that.

The war broke out around the time I was born, at the beginning of 1940. So I knew nothing other than war during my early years. I mean, when does your awareness of such things come into play? I remember certain scenes or events, the traumatic aspect of it at least, starting when I was about four years old. I remember the Nazi SS Colonel who used to stay, along with his men, at my grandmother's hotel, which was near the train station.

I can still see their uniforms, but I really don't remember a face. They were there, but all of them were faceless. I'm not even sure I ever looked at one of them straight on. I was probably too scared to do so. Yet I can see the profile, their uniforms and those long coats. I do see that. And they were so intimidating.

They used the hotel as a weekend stop. Our family used to get together there as well, because it was such a beautiful place with gardens all around. So the adults would play bocci ball and cards while the kids would play.

Like I said, I remember certain things. One day a couple of soldiers tossed two hand grenades out the window. They weren't necessarily trying to hit anybody. They had been drinking, and they were just fooling around. Fortunately, the grenades didn't hit anyone directly, although one of my cousins was hit by some shrapnel. But it was the trauma of it all that I most remember. There is this hole in the ground, and you're hearing the women screaming. When you hear your parents scream or see that kind of look on their faces, you know something is wrong.

At that time there were also lists, kind of like hit lists. My father was always afraid because for no reason, even if you weren't involved in politics or anything like that, they would nab you. The German soldiers would show up in a jeep, usually about three or four of them. Later, my dad told me he had 30 hand grenades hidden in his bedroom. He told me that if they had come for him, there would have been hell to pay. We never knew that.

Fear can be described in many different ways. If I was afraid, actually scared of getting in a race car, I would never do it. In this business it's important to have a healthy concern about the inherent dangers. I have to be realistic and aware of the fact that the worst can happen because that possibility is always there. I can either try to prevent it, try to see the situation before it happens, or avoid positioning myself where a major mistake can happen.

But my ultimate concern has more to do with the process than with the result. And that became so real recently, with the deaths of Ayrton Senna and Roland Ratzenberger. Clearly, those were situations caused by equipment failure, where neither one could have done anything to help themselves no matter what skills they possessed.

And that's happened to me. In fact, if I ever wake up at night, which I do sometimes, the dream, or nightmare, involves something where I'm no longer in control.

The scariest ones are those that have happened at super speedways, where an equipment failure occurred and suddenly I was just a passenger. It's the most helpless feeling in the world. You're just riding and then, boom. While it's happening, it's a terrible sensation. I've been very lucky in that regard, but that's also how I have been injured in this business. As a matter of fact, any injury I've had has come as a result of an equipment failure. If you fear anything, those are the things you fear because you know they are beyond your control.

I'm lucky that I've always been with good teams, so I know every-thing humanly possible is done to keep things safe. But there is always the possibility of something breaking, the specter of suddenly losing control. So from my perspective, it's concern rather than fear. I accept the fact that it's a calculated risk. I know I'm not going into totally uncharted waters where maybe I'll come out of it and maybe I won't. I am aware of the risk level and I know we are testing acceptable limits.

But once in the race car, your thoughts shift to the job at hand. You become focused on all the elements you can control. Your mind is so completely directed to a single purpose that any fears or concerns are forced into the background.

I have always understood the risks, but I really didn't want to acknowledge them. And I certainly didn't want to dwell on them. It was never something I would go into a corner and meditate about. I think if I had focused that much on the danger, there would have been no way in my own mind I could have rationalized stepping back into a car.

But fear is such an inner thing. Jackie Stewart, for example, retired right after his teammate, Francois Cevert, was killed at Watkins Glen. Guys that just walked away from the sport must have been motivated to do so by something.

I can't think of it being anything but fear. Again, I could never speak for anyone on something so private. I can only assume that is what it was.

My parents didn't know about our racing. My mother was pretty smart, so she had an idea. But there was no way to reason with my father on that issue, so my mom never said a word. I mean, we were still underage. Aldo and I were only 19 when he crashed at Hatfield. In those days you had to be 21 to obtain a racing license, so we had lied from the beginning.

It was the last race of the 1959 season, which was special for a couple reasons.

I had already qualified for the main event, and Aldo was in position to do the same. He was running third, and since the top five finishers in the heats qualified, there was no problem. But he was attacking like crazy. I remember hoping he would slow down.

In those days, they used to have a guardrail made of wood planks. But the planks didn't totally match up at the post, so you would have one sticking out

best. Aldo ended up hitting his head on the post, and as it turned out, he had a fractured skull.

So by the time we got to him on the track he was just lying there. As I say, there isn't a worse thing in your life you could ever see than your own brother lying unconscious. Our parents didn't know and there was nothing I could do. God, it was the end of the world for me.

The police chief from Hatfield Township

Although Aldo and I had been alternating in the same car all season, we had won enough races to be invited to the season-ending invitational. So the night of the accident was going to be the first time we had ever raced against one another. Aldo was going to drive our car and I was going to drive for somebody else.

here and there. When Aldo brushed against that guardrail, he caught the wheel on one of the exposed planks. It snapped him around, and the car went end over end. It was awful. By the time we got to him, he was out.

That season we had one helmet, a used helmet. Since we were alternating in the car, I'd have to borrow it every time I would run a race, and Aldo would do the same. The helmet fit, but it wasn't the

was investigating the accident. He had to file a report on it and sort of detected that maybe we weren't 21. I remember him asking me, 'How old is this boy?' He was looking at the license and you could tell, if you looked closely, that we had it fudged. I said, 'He's my twin. We're both 21.' But he knew. And I was just shaking. He says, '21, huh? All right.' That's what he wrote down.

I remember calling my mother. I said, 'Mom, I was racing and Aldo was watching me and he fell off the back of a pickup truck. He got the wind knocked out of him, and he's in the hospital. But we'll be home in the morning.' That's exactly what I said to her. And she was silent on the other end. The fact that we didn't go home that night, I mean, that was something for her to explain to my dad anyway. She didn't know what to say.

the following morning, the situation hadn't changed with Aldo. So the doctor came over and said, 'I expect this boy's parents here today. If not, we will have to call the police.' I said, 'No, no. I will call them.' You see, I was hoping he was going to wake up, we'd go home and everything would be fine.

But the day I had to tell my parents to come down, that was tough. I had to face the music then. At first, my father was so

I really think what brought Aldo around was talking to him about the new race car we were building. I would sit there talking racing to him. That's all. Just sitting by the bed and talking to him.

Finally, he opened his eyes, and you could tell he wanted to express himself. But it was several days before he could actually talk. The first words he said were, 'I'm glad you had to be the one to face the old man.' When Aldo said that,

Meanwhile, our buddies had loaded the car onto a flatbed truck and headed back to Nazareth. When they got there, they stopped at one of the local hangouts on Main Street.

Obviously, the car was destroyed and the word went out like wildfire. And they were talking about the worst, too. Now

despondent. His emotions got in the way, the proud man that he is. He said, 'You did this against my will,' things like that. Until then, I had never seen my father with tears in his eyes. It was a terrible time.

Aldo was in a coma for two or three weeks. So I would commute back and forth every day from Nazareth to Hatfield.

I figured now we have him back. He knew I had been the one that got bounced around the room like a football.

I'm sure my father thought, 'I've been mad. But, the boy is all right. And it's all over.'

It was just the beginning.

The only way I can describe the lack of safety in those early years is that we'd sit there at the driver's meeting at the beginning of the season and look around the room wondering who would be left at the end. It was like going to war.

That was a terrible part of my career that even now is hard to talk about. I mean, there were two sprint car races in the same year where we lost four guys, two in each race. And I was running in each of them. The first accident happened at Reading, where we lost Red Riegel and Jud Larson, a very good friend of mine, the same night.

Then about seven months later, we were in Gardena at Ascot Speedway. Two guys right next to me, my teammate Dick Atkins and Don Branson, were killed in the same accident. Two races, four deaths.

To be honest, I don't know how or why I accepted that kind of risk. Now that I reflect upon it, a lot of what happened doesn't make sense. But what kept you going was the idea that accidents happened every day on the road. You thought, I could be on my way to work and see my neighbor in an accident. What am I going to do, sell the car? Not go to work? What do you do? Does life stop there? No, it doesn't.

But there was a helluva price to pay in those days. A lot of the top midget stars of ARDC, which was the club I ran, guys like Tony Bonadias and "Dutch" Shaefer, they were all gone. I mean, these were guys that had 30-year careers. It was just amazing. That period, the 1950s and 1960s, really was the worst, when you look back on it.

The 1930s and 1940s were dangerous, but the speed wasn't quite there in that era. When you got into the '50s and '60s, technology had increased speeds tremendously but safety hadn't kept pace.

I remember one race, the first time I drove dirt cars at Langhorne, that really made me stop and think about the dangers that racing presented.

Langhorne had been lethal. There had been a number of drivers lost on that track, and no matter how focused you were on the race, you couldn't ignore the reality of that place. That was 1964, and I had been promised a ride with Dean Van Lines, which was going to be my first high-quality Indy Car team. But Al Dean didn't want me to drive at Langhorne because he had lost his primary driver, Jimmy Bryant, the year before on that same track.

But I picked up a ride and thought, well, I can't let that stop me. Langhorne might have been considered the toughest dirt track in the country, but I had to find out for myself.

Although I was able to sleep the night before the race, I remember having a feeling that I never wanted to experience again. That was the only time in my life where I wasn't really sure whether or not I'd come back. I knew if I could relax that night, then I'd be able to sleep through anything the rest of my life.

The next day I was a little uptight from fighting this feeling inside. My mechanic, Tommy Hinnershitz, was one of the top dirt racers on the East Coast. I mean, the guy was a hero on those kinds of tracks. And he's probably more responsible for saving my skin that day than anyone because of what he told me before qualifying.

Langhorne was shaped like a "D," so you could really get some momentum coming off the straightaway. But that was the problem because as you entered the corner, the radius became progressively tighter. You didn't realize that until you were well into the turn, which is how a lot of drivers got into trouble. Since the guardrail wasn't very high, guys would just flip over. And if you flipped in those cars, that was about it.

So Tommy told me in qualifying, 'When you come down on the back straightaway, look for the light pole. Everybody feels good at that point because you really get cooking there. But no matter how good it feels, back off.'

Without that advice I would have gone way beyond the pole, no question. Even then, for a second I thought, oh the hell with it. Then I decided no, I better not. That knowledge might have saved my life.

But I never had that feeling about a race track again. Ultimately, I think the experience was a positive one because I thought, this is about as bad as it's going to get, and I handled it.

By the way, that was the last race they had there on the dirt. The following year the track was paved and I set the world record for a mile track.

If you fear anything, you fear for your children. On one hand, I'm happy that Michael and Jeff are involved. I'm proud of them and I want to see them do well.

But there's one negative that never goes away. It's the danger, the fear that something could happen to one of them. Let's face it, that's the downside of the sport, the one aspect of our profession that doesn't change with time. Then to see it happen to Jeff like it did in 1992 at Indianapolis, the feeling I had was indescribable. I mean, he was so young and it was so early in his career. And it was all through no fault of his own.

That's why I consider that day to be the saddest of my career and easily the most emotionally draining. I had been the first one injured that afternoon. After hitting the wall, I ended up with some broken toes and bones in my feet. But my injuries were minor, things you knew in time would heal. Jeff's injuries were different, and because of their severity, you didn't know for sure what the outcome would be.

I was in the hospital waiting to be serviced, my feet packed in ice, when all of a sudden I heard a tremendous commotion. Everyone was moving around and getting prepared because there had been another accident. At the time, no one was saying anything to me. Finally, a doctor came over and said, "It's Jeff and it looks serious."

At that moment, what I feared the most was happening. All through life I had seen a lot of awful things happen to friends. As a driver, you sympathized with his family, and deep down, when you were alone and away from the track, you thanked the man upstairs that it didn't happen to you. And when it didn't, you knew you got away with it for another day.

But this time it hit the family and there was nothing anyone could do. Helpless. That's the only way I can describe the way I felt when they brought Jeff into the hospital. It's more awful than you can imagine because your first instinct is to do something, anything, to help. But then you realize you're at the mercy of other people and fate. It's a terrible feeling.

Jeff's car broke a hub and lost a wheel, which caused the car to do a 360 before hitting the wall nearly head-on. He sustained 48.9 Gs of impact, a remarkable amount considering anything approaching 50 Gs is about as much as a body will sustain before there are internal injuries. The cars have G meters, and with the use of microfilm, General Motors estimated the impact of the crash based on the speed and angle.

So the poor kid really went through a helluva shock. The car, from the front of the windscreen onward, was gone. That's why his legs were virtually shattered.

What made the situation even worse for Dee Ann and me was that everybody was so frantically involved with taking care of Jeff that no one took the time to give us any kind of report. In retrospect, I'm sure they were thinking, 'Right now, we've got a job to do. We'll worry about those things later.' But we had no idea how bad the situation was. When things finally settled down, we were left praying and hoping for the best. Jeff ended up spending eight and a half hours in surgery.

Meanwhile, out on the track, Michael was leading the race and leading strong. But by that point, the doctors had given me some pain pills so I ended up dozing off.

When I woke up, I realized Jeff was still in the operating room and the race was long over. I tried to check on him, but nobody was talking to me. So I'm worried about Jeff, but at the same time looking for something, anything, positive. I remember thinking, 'I know the race is over so somebody should at least be congratulating me.' I had remembered that Michael was still leading when I dozed off.

Finally, I saw a nurse, found out about Jeff, and then asked if the race was over. She said, 'Oh, yes.' But when I asked who had won, she asked, 'Are you sure you want to know?'

Michael's car had dropped out with 11 laps to go.

That was the worst day of my life.

I don't have any real superstitions, no routines or rituals that I make sure to follow. But one thing you'll notice is that I enter a race car the same way you would mount a horse, always on the left. You will never ever see me either approach or exit from the right side. I've never done it. Why? I don't know. It's just one of those things, and I'll go out of my way to make it happen. It really doesn't mean anything. But what does a superstition mean anyway? Nothing.

Just because something has gone their way on a particular day, some people get caught up in superstitions. But I've always thought it was totally counterproductive. When it becomes a crutch, suddenly you have something as stupid as that interfering with, or ruining, your mind-set.

Then again, it's widely known that I will not sign an autograph in green ink. Why? I don't know. But I'll take somebody else's pen if I'm handed one with green ink. It's stupid. I know it's 100 percent stupid. But that's the way it is.

Carl Haas goes through a whole ritual before a race. I've never understood it, but because it's something personal to him, I respect it. He'll chew on his cigar, and if you win the race, that cigar will go into a special box. He puts the name of the race on the cigar, and he might use it again for a particularly big event. Now if you don't do well, then the cigar gets pitched. I mean, he goes on and on. But that's the way he is.

And you know, it's all a part of the Carl I have come to admire and respect. He has had a tremendous impact on my career both personally and professionally. I spent 12 years with him, which is a lifetime in this sport, and I've found that deep down he truly has a heart of gold. Carl and his wife, Berni, have become very close with Dee Ann and me. The loyalty and friendship he has shown me over the years is something I will never forget.

The same is true of Paul. We have an absolutely unconditional friendship. If I had to count my closest friends, the ones that without any question are there and will be there through the rest of my life, they would fit on the fingers of one hand and Paul would be one of them. That's how I feel about both of them.

There is no question I had a fear of staying too long. The issue was always trying to judge the proper time. I didn't want to overstay my welcome, but I also didn't want to leave anything on the table. And that's a close one, a tough one to figure. In fact, I'll never really know how close I cut it.

But I always knew I didn't want to experience the alternative. I didn't want to find out that all of a sudden, not only wasn't I as effective as I had been, but I clearly wasn't the driver I used to be.

That would have stayed with me long after I left, and I couldn't afford to do that to myself. What I've noticed in reflecting upon my career is that all that keeps coming up are positives.

Could it have been that perfect? Hell no. Actually, the majority has probably been negative. But the positives were so overpowering, that's what I remember.

So for me to be able to go on with my life, I had to know that I didn't drag it out to the point that it got embarrassing or frustrating, which it easily could have if I stayed too long.

But it's such a fine line.

It was important to know that in my last season I still brought something to the team, that the mechanics still wanted to work with me. So when we started out well in Australia, there was no way it could end up a total negative. When that first race went well, I almost considered it mission accomplished.

What I do know is that if I had walked away any earlier, I would have been miserable. What scares me most about making the decision to leave is that nothing else really excites me. Nothing turns me on like I'm used to being turned on by motor racing. Am I going to be so antsy that I can't stand it? I don't know. Maybe I'll put that energy to good use in another environment. But I don't know where I'm going to channel that drive.

My whole adult life I haven't known anything else. In that respect it will be a major adjustment.

I hope I don't go out and kill myself in a damn boat or something else away from my work, something totally meaningless just to satisfy those old desires.

I had a feeling inside that the time was right, but I'll never know for sure.

In order for me to succeed, I needed to be serene, to have a clear mind. I needed to have peace back home, where things are important to me. I had to be

sure that everything was fine with the family. Any disruption there would have played hell with the mental side of my work. It could have destroyed me because I'm very fragile. I really am. A lot of

things bother me. The unfortunate thing is I'm like an open book. I show my emotions a lot. So as a parent and a husband I had to do what felt good to me. That focus was a natural thing. It wasn't forced. I mean, I was doing it for selfish reasons to some degree. But you see, I wanted to have it all.

My father was an orphan when he was five and was raised by a priest, Father Quirino Ghersa, who later lived with us. My uncle-priest, as I called him, spoke fluent German and helped keep us together through the war.

Ultimately, I think he was the one that saved my dad because even among the Nazis, there was still some respect for the church. With his connections and ability to speak the language, my uncle-priest was able to work politically to help keep us together on our way to Lucca.

Other than my parents, he was the person I felt the most affection for all through my youth. There was something about the guy. He had this goodness about him, but he was not "holier than thou." He was a good Catholic priest, and he was very tolerant, especially with kids.

We used to go to confession and tell our sins—lies, things like that. The old-time priests, to set an example, would have you say a rosary. But the longest line was always for my uncle-priest because he would give a lighter penance, maybe two Hail Marys, something like that.

I used to go to him and talk through the screen. I wouldn't think he knew who I was. He knew. But he'd act like he didn't know. He was such a great guy.

When we left Italy to come over to the States, we left behind a lot of close family members like my grandparents, whom I loved dearly. But he was the one that was the toughest to leave. You know how kids are about writing? I wasn't the greatest writer, but I always kept in touch with him.

And that's why having mass before every race means so much to me. Father Phil DeRea, who is a missionary of the Sacred Heart, has become a very close friend of the family, and he usually says a short mass either before or after the driver's meeting.

Most of the time it's done inside the trailer, although we have moved the ceremony to the garage in recent years at Indianapolis. Given the way I felt about my uncle-priest, it's very comforting to have such a strong relationship with Father Phil. He really has a special way about him, an ability to help you make sense of everything going on around you.

I'm not sure I could survive properly without the balance my faith gives me. And Father Phil is a large part of that.

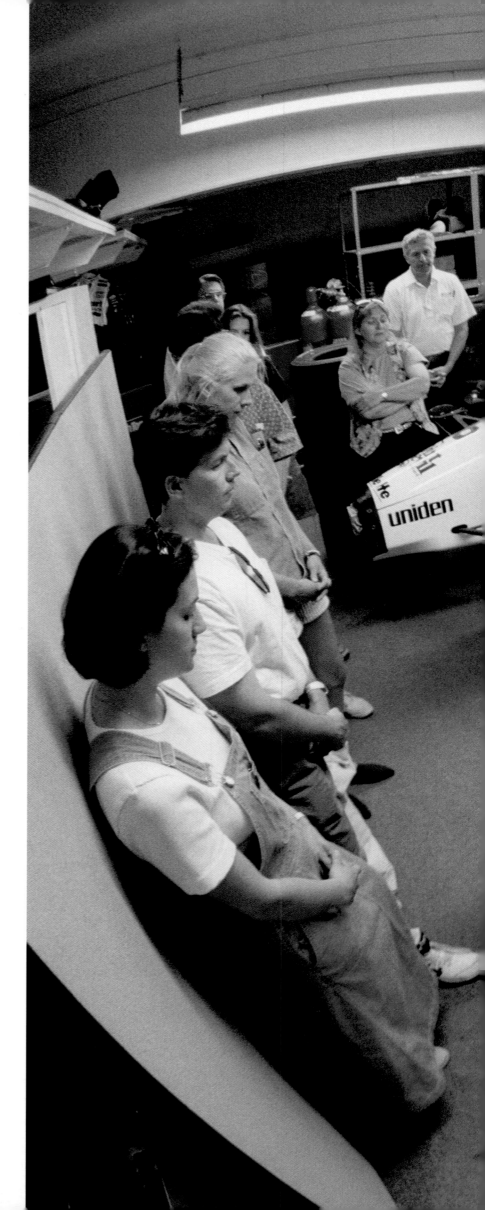

You have a variety of emotions, a roller coaster of emotions, when your sons are involved in racing. Number one, what comes to mind as a parent, as a father, is the safety aspect. Obviously, this sport can be violent and we know that.

We also know that if you're going to compete, you have to do so with your eyes wide open. And yet, even though I understand there is a calculated risk, I am left with the knowledge my sons are taking that risk.

Do I support them? Yes. Why? Because that's what they wanted to do. I am guilty of having exposed them at such an early age. But they could have gone any way at all and I would have supported them. They chose motor racing.

I'm sure it was the same way with my nephew, John. But once they decided, obviously, as their fathers, Aldo and I were going to help them. Then to see them succeed, you have nothing but pride.

At first, when I found myself racing against them, I thought, dammit, these kids should have a little more respect. But they don't. I think Michael, more than Jeff or John, has made some passes on me for the lead. I mean, it's tough enough to compete against other drivers, but do I have to breed them too? But then you think, well, there's a little bit of me there. You realize some of your blood is flowing through those veins.

The more you see that, and I've been lucky enough to see quite a bit, the more proud you are. Believe me, if I were losing to Michael or Jeff, I'd still enjoy the sport.

In the beginning, Dee Ann had the reaction of every normal wife in the world. She would say, 'What's the matter with you? Are you crazy?' When it all cooled down she would just shake her head. I think Dee Ann's the one that has always understood what this means to us.

Since we had children quite young, there has never been a generation gap with my kids. Even with my grandchildren, we can play the same games together. And that's what keeps us close as a family. I bought the "toys" for them, but I liked them first. In fact, I justified buying them because I knew I would enjoy them as much as they would.

With my father and me it was different, but not in a negative way. I have always looked up to him. And now that we are older, I admire him even more for all that he has done to make my life what it has become. He's a warm, wonderful man. And when it's all said and done, I hope my kids feel the same way about me.

I was always drawn to airplanes. I love them, I really do. And they have been very important to my career in terms of the longevity I have been able to enjoy. Also, there is no way I would have been able to do all the different events early in my career.

If I would have had to take commercial flights from Terre Haute, Indiana, one night to a sprint car race in Ohio the next night, for example, I would have missed a lot of opportunities. So it's been a wonderful tool for my work.

Over the years, I've owned several planes. Now, with Michael's earning power, we have been able to combine our resources and move up to a Lockheed Jet Star. That was an important upgrade, particularly when Michael was competing in Formula One in 1993.

I have always had my planes flown professionally. If I had flown myself, the convenience factor would have disappeared. Obviously, it's not like you jump in the car, head to the airport, board the plane, and take off. There are a number of logistical considerations. But owning airplanes has definitely improved my quality of life and helped extend my career.

My daughter Barbie's boyfriend and his brother decided to get a pig for an aunt out in Kansas. Well, the aunt didn't think having a pig around was so funny.

So Barbie called and told us how cute the pig was, and she got Dee Ann all excited about keeping it. I said, 'No way. Absolutely not.' So we made a deal. I would try to find it a home, but he couldn't stay for more than two weeks because we also had a Great Dane.

Eventually, I called Barbie and told her I had found a place. But by then, she had already found him a home. So I thought, closed chapter, right? Two weeks later we get a call from the airport and we're told there's a pig waiting for us. He's in a pig taxi, which looks like one of those doggie boxes. Dee Ann had arranged to get another one. I was fit to be tied.

But the pig was so funny because he was just oblivious of everything around him. The dog had a pretty big dish he would eat out of. And he was big enough that the pig, Barbie named him Martini, could walk right under him and eat anything that came out of the bowl. It got to the point that the dog wouldn't spill a single crumb. Nothing would come out of that bowl. It was funny watching the two coexist.

When the dog came in for the last time at night we would give him a little treat. He'd go into the cage, and that would be it. So Martini was noticing all this. And one night I gave the dog a treat and the pig jumped up, grabbed it out of his mouth, and ran into the dog cage. The poor dog was looking around like, 'What the hell happened?'

I think Martini probably caused the dog to leave us a couple months before he would have otherwise.

But I get a kick out of Martini. I mean, what the hell are you going to do with a pig? It's doomsday if you give him to a farm because he's going to be bacon the next day. I just can't let myself do that. Unfortunately, I'm the only one resisting. My wife would give him away in a minute. I mean, he's not too handy and he's not the easiest animal to have around. He's not good with kids, or Barbie for that matter. They don't get along because he actually went after her once.

So I guess you could say he's really not a "people" pig. But here I am with the pig. And you know, when we're alone together, just Martini and myself, we get along fine.

The day we sailed into New York Harbor, June 16, 1955, was my sister Anna Maria's 21st birthday. At 5:00 in the morning, we were in front of the Statue of Liberty. It was a beautiful day, not a cloud in the sky.

My cousin John picked us up in New York in a Plymouth station wagon, and we drove to Nazareth, our new home. In those days, the roads were not as good as they are now, so it took us about two hours. But we stopped for lunch at one of those shiny 1950s diners.

That's when I had my first milkshake. The food? All I can tell you is that it was nothing like my mother's cooking. I remember thinking that everything tasted like cardboard. I'm not sure what we had, but even my father thought it was awful. The milkshake was the only passable thing. I thought, man, I'm going to have to live on milkshakes for the rest of my life.

That was probably the biggest shock, the food, and the only negative I can remember. Everything else had a glimmer of hope.

When Michael was little, we had a neighbor that was building go-carts for his son. So we got Michael going in that direction. And this was something very normal, not out of the ordinary.

But it was like Little League, where parents were coming up to me saying, 'He bumped my kid, he did this or that.' I had a helluva time trying to keep everybody cool. I had to put out a lot of fires.

But his approach was just unmistakable. First of all, you try to tell him all about safety. You didn't want your boy hurt. I mean, I had to answer to my wife, and she wasn't all that thrilled about it. But he was just a natural.

I felt a little bit guilty because I was making available to him everything I would have loved to have had when I was a kid. *Everything.* And he seemed to snap it up just like I would have. As you might expect, it pleased the hell out of me to see him react that way. When he won his first national go-cart race he was actually too young for his class.

Michael's next big move into racing came when he was 16. I had a good friend, Andre Pilette, who owned a driving school in Belgium, and he took on Mike and John for about 10 days. It was a great experience because they had the undivided attention of Andre. These kids took full advantage and ended up breaking all the student records. So the signs where there. And everywhere Michael went, he won a championship.

Before he progressed into Indy Cars, I let him take a couple of laps in my car at Elkhart Lake in 1983. Immediately, he was approaching competitive times. I knew the car was working well and safe, but he was right into it.

was the second son and he pretty much followed in Michael's footsteps. He accomplished a lot of the same things, but it took him a little more time. Jeff is much more laid back, so he's much tougher to read.

Ultimately, when Jeff got comfortable, he won just like Michael. He actually stayed in go-carts a little longer than Michael, and consequently, won more races. Then we enrolled him in Skip Barber's driving school, and he was very successful. As with Michael, Jeff was well prepared and you could see he had talent.

Jeff won his share of races coming up through the ranks, but the real difference came when he was ready to graduate to Indy Cars. Jeff's team wasn't nearly as strong as Michael's had been at the start of his Indy Car career. There was nowhere near the commitment to Jeff, and that's where he suffered.

To be honest, even in the IRS series he never really had good strong backing. So sometimes I took responsibility for the cars and crashes. And a couple times we took some pretty good hits financially.

Unfortunately, I think Jeff always felt a responsibility for that. So during those formative years he drove with a cloud over his head. As much as I tried to not have him think about it, he knew. He's very sharp and he didn't want to be costing me money.

But sometimes when you race with that hanging over you, you can't be yourself. I think he probably made some mistakes he wouldn't have made if he had the freedom Michael enjoyed.

So for Jeff it's been an unfair situation. That's why all along I've felt the jury is out as far as his ultimate capabilities. I don't think Jeff has shown what he's capable of doing yet. I pray to God that he has that opportunity before long because it would be very important all-around.

To this day, even if she just comes home to visit for a few days, it's a breath of fresh air when Barbie's around. I mean, that's when everything comes alive because she's so energetic.

When we go up to our place in the Poconos, everything is out. Nothing is left untouched when she is there. And I love it. We can go waterskiing, then run over and play tennis. She's unstoppable. But when she leaves, it's like a morgue around there. Barbie's got a lot of life. And she brings out the kid in me because I like to play hard and she holds nothing back.

The kids have all had their own goals. Their minds were set very early in life. Take Barbie, for example. When she was a toddler, she was introduced to equestrian competition through her cousin Caroline, Aldo's daughter.

Caroline had an appaloosa she used to show. There was a class where they put little toddlers on the horse, paraded them around, and the kids would get a ribbon.

Well, that was Barbie. It was just like racing was for me. She snapped right onto the competition, and before you know it I'm providing her with horses. And she went right up to national level.

We got to the point where we had several horses, including one we brought over from New Zealand. Eventually, I started putting some reality into what was happening. She knew the hard work. It's no different than a world-class skater wanting to become an Olympian.

For anything like that, you've got to set aside a big chunk of your life. And here was a girl who, as a young teenager, was on her own every weekend. She would set her alarm for three in the morning and get up all by herself.

A lot of those kids had parents that wanted their children competing in that environment. But Barbie was doing it all on her own. She had a ride to the farm where she prepared her horse and then traveled 150 or 200 miles with the trainer to show. She did everything flat out.

Eventually, I said, 'Barbie, when you look at the sport, you have to look at the compensation side of it. Let's face it, there is not a helluva lot of money to be made.

'At most there are two or three trainers in the world that make real money. You either have to get deep into it or out of it.' So eventually she said, 'You know Dad, I like horses, but I want to be a singer.'

I thought, 'Oh no.' But you know, that's great because she's not afraid of competition. Whether she will succeed in becoming a world-class pop singer, who knows?

But the goal is there and she's got the guts. She *does* have the guts, I'll tell you that. Sooner or later, somebody is going to see that. She has probably chosen the most competitive field in the world. But she's not afraid.

Naturally I'm behind her and I'll do whatever I can to help. I'm lucky that at least she has a dream. And from my own life, I know perseverance usually pays off.

With so many races over so many years, the highs and lows came and went with the wind. But all along the way, Dee Ann never wavered. She provided a balance to my life that helped make my career possible. Whether I was walking through the bright lights of Victory Lane or shuffling through the shadows of defeat, Dee Ann was always the same. Not only did her strength give me the stability I needed at home, but she allowed me the freedom to chase my dreams.

And for the most part, particularly early in my career, I took advantage of that latitude. In many ways, I was very selfish because I put racing ahead of everything else. If there was an open date in the schedule and somebody wanted me to drive, I was gone. There were no weekends to ourselves because there were no weekends off.

But where others might have demanded I cut back or at least complained about all the time away, Dee Ann never once said, 'What about me?' I know she sacrificed a lot on my behalf, and I know I couldn't have done any of this without her.

It's nothing you plan, nothing you can look down the road and see. It's just the character of a special person that makes it all work.

I remember when I was traveling in Europe in the 1970s and early 1980s. It got to the point that when the whole family traveled, it was a hassle for all the obvious reasons. I told Dee Ann, 'Look, the kids are at the age now where they can be left at home if you're traveling with me. Or, if you don't want to travel, I'll take them one at a time.'

It only happened a couple times, but those were the memorable trips. I remember Jeff and Mike both being at races where I won. We were like pals. Jeff was a great companion. Michael was a little more demanding, but that was fine, too. I remember being in Holland

at the Dutch Grand Prix and Jeff was along. I took him to the parties after the race so he could be a part of it all. Just he and dad together. Those are the things that you remember.

You can take all the trips and put them away in one little box. But those, the ones with the kids, you keep outside on display. That one-on-one is what is memorable.

I never had that with my father. I mean, I never had a real one-on-one, heart-to-hear conversation with my father at that age. I love my father dearly, but we didn't have tha kind of relationship. The times were just much different.

My father had owned seven farms, and from the town square, which was up on a hill, you could look in one direction and almost as far as you could see was my father's property. He used to export grains, grapes, everything. So he was at the point where he could have been well-off the rest of his life. And then it was all taken away. I really don't know for sure how his life was spared.

When the war ended, the borders were in dispute, as they always are following war. The peninsula of Istria, which was where our town, Montona, was located, became part of Yugoslavia. So for a while, we were trapped inside a Communist country.

But soon after, we became part of a mass of people crossing into Italy. And Italy had to accept us because we wanted to maintain our citizenship.

And all these refugees, which is what we had become, were funneled into disbursement camps. Whatever you could carry, you loaded up on huge transporters. You took the most valuable pieces from your home. I mean, invaluable pieces like grandfather clocks.

But when we arrived at the border checkpoint, there was nowhere to put everything, so you ended up losing all that, too. All you had was what clothing you could put into suitcases.

Obviously, not everybody could get through that checkpoint at once, so for a variety of reasons all the males went to one side and all the females went to the other. For days, I didn't see my mother or my sister. As kids, we didn't really know what was happening.

But I could see how it was affecting my parents. I mean, my dad was a guy that had everything in place and it all had crumbled. We had gone through the war and we were all alive. Then this happens. It was the end of the world for him. But he kept his morale up with a lot of strength and a strong belief in his nationality.

We ended up at the border in Udine for about two weeks. It was awful. There were maybe 3,000 or 4,000 people. We had other family there with us, but we were all split up. Eventually we were moved to Lucca. You had to go. It wasn't like you had a choice.

But Lucca was beautiful, charming. The town and the surroundings were in a very beautiful part of Italy called Tuscany. Lucca was within 30 kilometers of beautiful beaches at the beginning of the Italian Riviera.

We only had one room and we shared bathrooms with other families. All of this was supposed to be temporary, but we ended up being there seven years.

I can assure you that as kids we were never hungry. We never suffered in that respect. We had what we needed; my father always saw to that. Yes, there was modesty, but we went on. And my dad maintained his dignity, and we all pulled together.

But that experience, as bad as it was at times, taught me to appreciate the simple things in life.

As a result, I think I've enjoyed life a lot more. I have found that some people can have everything humanly possible, and they become bored. Just look at a kid, for example. You give him a dip of ice cream, and he'll kill for another one. Give him a big bowl, and he'll never touch it. That's how it is in life. If you have everything available, there's nothing to look forward to.

To me, half of the appreciation is the anticipation. And I think this is something my kids have missed. They have maintained their values and they have good character, but their lives have been nothing like mine.

I'm richer because I have had those experiences.

I used to be able to go so hard to get a lap time in qualifying.

Other guys would say, 'How the hell did you get that lap?' I didn't know. I just went for it. Some of that is not there anymore. I want it, but it's not there. Why? I don't know. Maybe it's because I've been in it so long that I know the possible consequences if I miss. All those things are signs to tell you that you've had enough.

When my dad said we were going to America, Aldo and I were 15. We were already messing around with cars, and, naturally, we had a lot of friends. At that time, I had as deep a love for motorcycles as I did for cars. If I had stayed in Italy, that's probably what I would have become, a motorcycle racer. That would have made much more sense given the circumstances.

So Aldo and I were reluctant about leaving Italy. And we could also see some reluctance on the part of our parents.

When we left, I remember telling our grandparents, 'No tears. We'll be back.' In our own minds, we felt 100 percent certain we would return. The perception was that it might be easy to become wealthy in America, so you'd make money and go home.

The idea that we were not going permanently eased the way and helped make it less traumatic. Obviously, the world was not as small then as it is today. It took us eight days on the *Conte Biancamano* to reach New York from Genova.

We were not in first class by any means, but the accommodations were very acceptable. We first landed in Nova Scotia, where we had a day to go touring or whatever. I remember my father thinking us kids could speak English because we had taken it in school. Hell, we couldn't go anywhere. I couldn't even ask for a postcard. That's where reality set in as far as the language.

Back in Italy, my sister, Anna Maria, had gone on to further her education at the Art Institute in Lucca. She's still extremely creative and a very good artist.

So when we got settled in Nazareth, she picked up a job with one of the department stores as a window trimmer. My brother and I went on to school and we worked part-time. Actually, we alternated. He would go one day and I'd go the next.

We worked for my Uncle Louie, who had a gas station at the end of town in Nazareth. Not only were we making money, but more importantly, we had contact with people so we could learn the language. I had three years of English in Italy, and you learned grammar primarily.

So once we got into the practice of speaking, it was easy to grasp. I set a goal of being able to speak English with anybody by Christmas. And that's what I did.

By 1957, just two years after we arrived, my dad had enough money to build a new home and buy two cars. We had a brand new 1957 Chevy and a Buick Roadmaster. And everything paid for. That's what a lot of families did at that time. They pulled together by pooling all the resources, and as a result, they were able to get on their feet quickly.

It's hard to say, but I think Aldo was a better driver than I was before his accident at Hatfield. I mean, there is no reason for me to say I was better than him. I had nothing to show in that respect.

But as luck would have it, if anything was going to happen during a race, it seemed like it was always happening in front of him. It's amazing. Then in 1969 he had a serious accident, and that's when he decided for himself that he'd had enough.

It was tough not having my brother around anymore. In 1961, I had gone on to midgets and let him take over the stock cars. After a while, he got into midgets, then sprint cars. And he had some good races, but the sport was never really kind to him.

And that changed his life. We ended up taking two different paths, which was troubling for me because I knew how much it meant to him. We had grown up sharing the same dreams and he had been denied.

His life had to continue in a different way, in a different pattern. That's why I see him reliving a lot of it through his son John. I mean, in my opinion, no one knows or appreciates how much Aldo is behind John. I don't think John understands the depth of that support or how much he has done for Aldo by being successful. But I can see it.

I see Aldo beam when John is doing well. He's so proud of him when he's racing. I can see, ultimately, that this has become his satisfaction. Aldo is a very serene, happy guy. He's been successful, has a good business, a nice family. So it's not like life has not been good to him in that respect. He's just taken a different path and it's worked fine.

But I've thought about how things might have been different. How would his life have been? How would his career have been without that accident? We'll never know. But I like to speculate that it could have been much different.

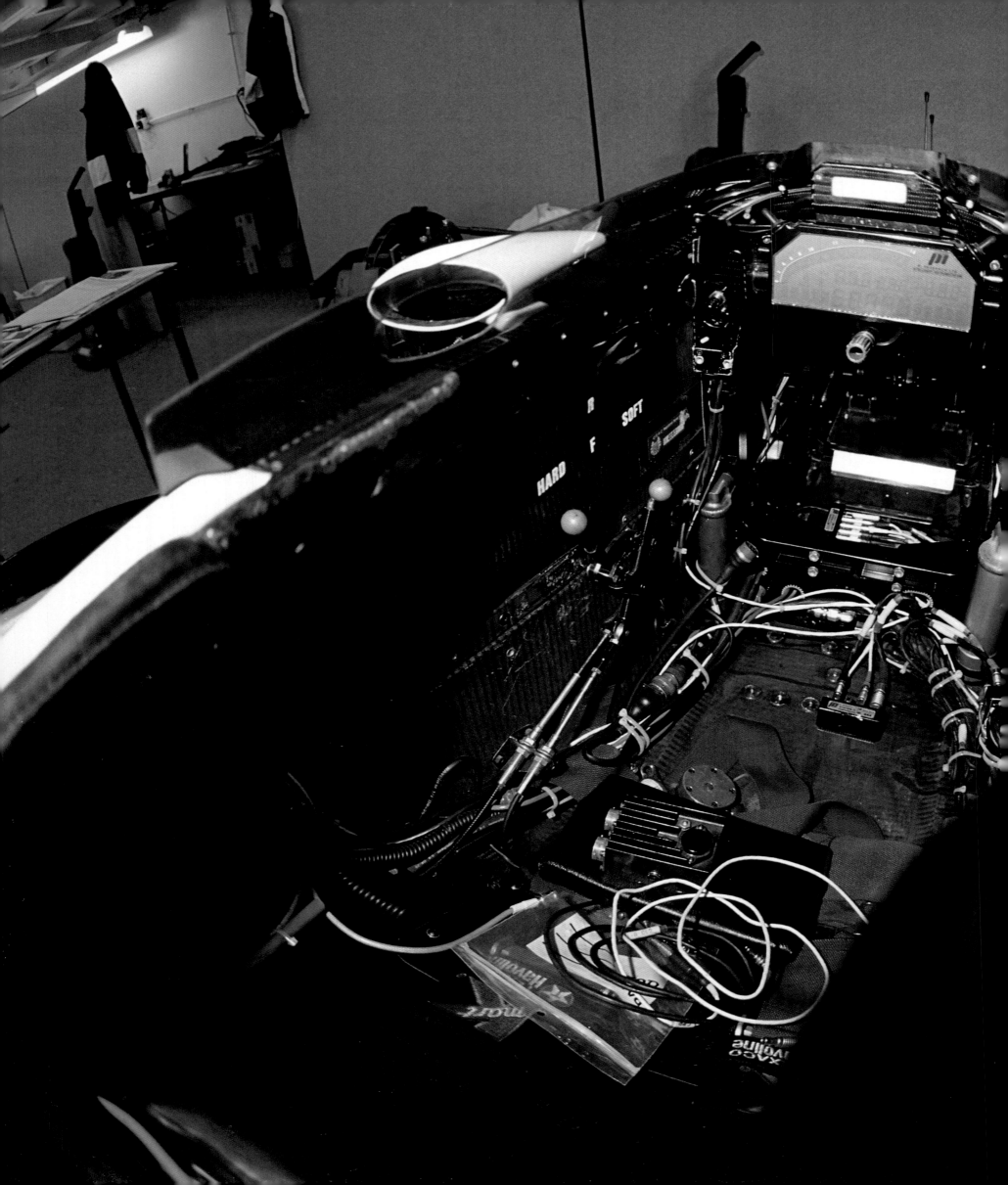

One fact about today's cars is that there are so many adjustments. Every time you go out, whether you're testing or at practice, you go with a different setup. And they are infinite.

There is the mechanical side and then there is the aerodynamic side. And it's so tough because the read is almost impossible at times.

With all the computers, you can analyze every aspect of the car, the G loadings and everything else, and still the situation isn't black-and-white.

We'll change what we call one flat on the spring platform. That's a mere 15,000ths of an inch, and it will make a difference in terms of balance. Sometimes that can mean two- to three-tenths of a second per lap.

You have no idea how close you are setting up the car. For balance, we'll change the wings a quarter of a degree. You know how much a quarter of a degree is? You can hardly see it move. But those are the differences. You can imagine how easy it is to be off.

I don't want to get too technical, but just to give you an idea of what we go through, you have damper loadings, and on the high-speed rebound, you have 600 or 700 pounds of force. You can make a change of just 15 pounds, which is less than three percent, and it will make a difference. And you'll feel it in the car. That's what you go through.

So you have to understand and keep up with the technology because obsolescence is the order of the day. By that, I mean there is always something with a new twist or turn that you've got to be aware of. It's a constant search.

If your car, or the tool of your trade, has limitations, no matter how skillful you are, there is only so far you can take it. But if you know how to extract more of what that piece of equipment has to give, then you can go that much further. From day one, a race car was always an adjustable tool. The more modern the car, the more adjustable it became.

Over the years, I really have had a fascination with the technology. A lot of the old-timers come up to me and say, 'Oh, for the good old days.' Well, to some degree, yes, you had a few more laughs. But to me, the good old days are right now. That's the way I've always felt. If you took the technical aspect out of racing, everything would have remained status quo and rather boring.

You want to go into uncharted waters where you don't know for sure what's on the other side.

My first midget ride came in this car with the Mataka Brothers. I have no idea why they painted a question mark on the side. Those two guys always were a little different. As it turned out, that car was significant because at that point in my career I was racing ARDC against the best midget drivers in the country. That's also the car I used to win three races in one day on Labor Day in 1963.

Our third car, the white No. 7, was a 1937 Hudson sedan. We had started out with a 1948 Hudson Hornet that Aldo crashed in Hatfield. Then we built a 1937 Hudson coupe, which also ended up being destroyed. So we built the sedan in one week by working around the clock. But we rushed it so much that a brake line got pinched during our first race with the car. As a result, I was out of brakes midway through, but ended up winning it anyway. I won about 12 races in that stock car in 1960.

I drove several races for Ford in this stock car in 1967, including Charlotte, Atlanta, Riverside, and Daytona. In fact, I won the Twelve Hours of Sebring and ran the 500 at Atlanta in the same weekend. Foyt and I were flying back and forth on the Ford plane so we could qualify for both races. Sebring was on Saturday and Atlanta was on Sunday. I was running third in Atlanta with about 10 laps to go when I blew a tire.

I won my first USAC sprint car race, the Pat O'Connor-Joe James Memorial, in 1964 at Salem, Indiana, in this car. It was a 100-lapper and a big win for me. I really believe that car helped get me a ride at Indianapolis because I was racing against the top Indy Car drivers, guys like A.J. Foyt and Don Branson, and I was finishing in the top three. The car wasn't exactly state-of-the-art, but it was good to me.

I shared this Ferrari with Chris Amon at Sebring. I won Sebring three times, the first in 1967 with Bruce McLaren.

This car was the only Ferrari ever entered in the Can-Am Series. And this particular race was at Watkins Glen in 1972. The car had a big seven liter Ferrari engine.

I ran the Lotus "78," which was the first ground effects car, during the 1977 Formula One season. In this race, the Dutch Grand Prix, which I started from the pole, I'm pretty sure I ended up crashing with James Hunt. But that was a great car.

There was a huge jump in speed in the early 1970s, when the first meaningful aerodynamics were introduced to single seaters. From then on, it's been fairly gradual. This car is the contemporary Lola.

I don't necessarily blame today's drivers because they didn't have the opportunities that were available years ago. But I think you can overcome that lack of experience with sheer determination and drive. It might not look very good at the beginning, but, ultimately, people will acknowledge that burning desire.

When I drove my first Indy Car I didn't even have a test. Not only had I never sat in an Indy Car, but I had never gone that fast. Although I had driven at Trenton, which was a mile track that allowed you to get up into the 180-mile-an-hour range, I had raced there in an inferior sprint car. But I had never gone that fast on that kind of surface in a situation where everything, including a new car, was thrown at me.

Then again, my preparation was nowhere as sophisticated as that of today. Mike, Jeff, and John are shining examples in terms of how knowledgeable they were by the time they broke into Indy Cars.

In my case, especially in the early days when I went to Daytona or Bridgehampton, I had no freaking idea what the hell I'd be dealing with. I mean, none.

It was just sheer absolute desire and guts that got me through. Of course, that's why the nights before those races would be hell because you didn't know what lay ahead. So you just came to understand that one way or another you would deal with it. There was nothing comfortable about that approach, but you were almost trying to psychologically fake your way through the process.

Sometimes I look back and I wonder, 'Was I lucky or crazy?' My first Indy Car ride was a good example of what went on in that era. I took over for Troy Ruttman, who stood about 6-4. Naturally, there was all kinds of room in that cockpit.

But I didn't dare say I didn't fit because someone would have said, 'What's the matter kid, are you too small to drive?' I never even considered pointing out something like that. I had been told before that I wasn't big enough or strong enough to drive.

So given my desire and the opportunity that car afforded me, I certainly wasn't worried about being bounced around a little bit.

When I started, the issue of safety had not been addressed. In midgets, for example, you didn't even have a shoulder harness. You had a lap belt and a strap to hold yourself in, but that's it. Even the roll bar was below your head.

And it was accepted. Pointing these things out or showing concern was not the macho thing to do. There is no question that as a result I've seen a lot of terrible things in the course of my career. And you start to ask questions. What can we do? Are we doing everything possible? No? Then why don't we do something?

So we started talking about it collectively. I like to take credit for really getting a lot of that going. I started putting padding and other things around the cockpit because there had never been anything there. I thought, 'What the hell good am I to myself if I'm not here to race tomorrow?'

In the beginning we saw front engine cars with just a little bit of a roll bar in the back. But because those cars had such a high center of gravity, they were very prone to flip. The driver was totally exposed, and that's how he would sustain most of his injuries.

Later, when we went to rear engine cars, you had a car much lower to the ground. It might spin and crash, but a significant portion of the impact would be absorbed by the wide suspension. What was the next problem? Fire.

The majority of the drivers killed during the late '60s through the mid '70s died because of fires. They would have survived the injuries.

My first rear engine car had the tube frame and two saddle tanks with 40 gallons on each side. Obviously, under impact the fuel would either burst at the fuel caps or explode at the seams. And they were just aluminum tanks. So the next problem was figuring out a way to contain the fuel.

Goodyear is probably the biggest supplier of the fuel bladders used in race cars today. The technology was developed in Vietnam for helicopters. They had to find something that could withstand gunfire because the enemy would shoot them down by firing at the tanks. So materials strong enough to sustain those kinds of blows were developed. Later, that technology was applied to race cars. Eventually, rules were created that moved all the fuel behind the driver.

However, the element of fire still didn't go away. Under the pressure of a huge impact, the car would separate, the tub from the engine. And when that happened, fuel lines broke and you had fire again. Everyone realized we had to have a quick disconnect, and that came from aviation technology. Whenever the two parts of the car would split, the fuel lines automatically sealed.

Though relatively slow, the progress has been dramatic. Just the changes that have been made since 1991 are significant. In 1992, Jeff was driving a 1991 model car for A.J. Foyt at Indianapolis. From 1991 to 1992 there were some safety improvements in the front end of the car. If Jeff had been in a current model car, it's possible his injuries would have been reduced by 30 or 40 percent. If he would have driven a 1993 model, probably another 20 percent would have been eliminated. If he had been in a 1994 car, with the same impact, he probably would have walked away from that crash.

All along, most people didn't want to hurt themselves. The ones that you respected, the ones that were there for the long pull, that's where the help came from with regard to safety issues. I remember in Europe there was no problem getting the attention of Jackie Stewart, who in his own way was very much involved.

But you have to understand that most of the safety features in a race car are performance penalties. So unless safety issues were regulated, where everyone had to abide by the same rules, it wouldn't work. You're not going to get anyone to voluntarily add 20 pounds to the car to make the driver more safe. An engineer wouldn't do that. Nobody would do that. You just couldn't afford to make those kinds of changes unilaterally, so you would go without them.

But that's where we got smarter.

The events that you longed for, the ones you thought, 'I've got to put this one under my belt,' those are the ones you remember. Then that feeling of driving into Victory Lane or crossing the finish line, it's indescribable. When you finally do put it under your belt, what a beautiful, beautiful relief. But it's more a sense of accomplishment because you know the importance and you did it. It's a tremendous payoff. It really is.

There are three key ingredients in this business—the equipment, the team, and the driver. If any one of those of elements is missing or not operating at a high level, then you're not going anywhere. A driver can create some fireworks with an inferior car, but he will not win regardless of how well he's capable of manipulating that machine. If the equipment is incapable of taking a driver to the top, skill alone will not get it done.

That's why my association with Newman/Haas has been so important to my career. Not only is the team and the equipment at the highest possible standards, but the relationship has provided a continuity that I think is missing with a lot of my contemporaries. Guys such as Johnny Rutherford and Al Unser Sr. still wanted to race and they probably could have accomplished more if they had the same opportunity I had. That's why I give the Newman/Haas Racing Team a lot of credit for my longevity. Results are what keep you going in this game, and Carl and Paul have helped make the positive results possible.

I won the World Championship in 1978, but winning the title in 1977 might even have been easier. In fact, I might have won more races because of all the events I was leading before various problems forced me to drop out.

There were several races where I was way ahead and never finished the race. South Africa was one. Colin Chapman, my boss, always wanted to give you that extra advantage if there was one.

For instance, he calculated the fuel in such a way that you would finish the race with no more than one liter left. And that was fine when it worked. But in those days the calculations weren't always black-and-white. The point is, I lost South Africa and I lost Sweden because he cut me so short.

In South Africa, which is at a high altitude, the car ran a lot leaner, so you didn't require as much fuel. But sure enough, with two laps to go, I'm leading the race and I run out of fuel.

The next time it happened was in Sweden. The fuel metering unit that determined the mixture somehow slipped into full rich. It was about midway through the race, and although I'm leading, I'm also thinking, 'I'm not going to finish because I know how short he cuts me on fuel.' Seven laps from the end, the thing ran dry.

In Canada, I had more than a lap lead when another problem developed. Because I had fluctuating oil pressure I was nursing it along in hopes of getting to the end. But on the last lap, I'm coming down the straightaway when the engine blows up and scatters all over the place. I tried to coast it in, but I was about 100 yards from the finish line when it stopped.

If I finish any one of those races, then I win the championship. So you are measured on what you don't accomplish. Yet, in those races I had it accomplished. You feel so cheated.

There are all these other elements and they have to work for you. When they don't, you feel cheated, and so do all the guys working on that car. And trying to maintain sanity is half the battle. It's the only individual sport where you can do everything right and still lose, where you can be completely prepared and end up without any results. But you have to accept that going in.

There is a much more broad-minded view of racing today compared to the early years of my career. NASCAR, for example, used to be so territorial. You had to have a southern drawl to feel like you belonged, and if you came from anywhere north of North Carolina you were considered a foreigner. Now you have guys such as Ernie Irvan, who is from California, and Rusty Wallace, who is from St. Louis, so there has been that acceptance. But in my era, not only was I from the North, but I wasn't even American-born. And I'm sure it didn't set well with everyone back then.

But there were bigger men running the show, guys such as "Big" Bill France. I had so much respect for that man. I had started running sports cars down in the 24 Hours of Daytona in 1966, so I had some recognition down there. When I talked to him about coming down and driving stock cars at Daytona, he really opened his arms. I'm not sure the rest of the community was quite as inviting, but he was, and that was important to me. I knew it took a long time to feel accepted, and I'm not sure I ever really was in those days. But anytime I go to a NASCAR race today, I really feel welcomed, and that's something I have come to truly appreciate.

But I'll never forget winning Daytona in 1967. I had come into the pits leading, and a representative from Ford nearly cost me the race. Fred Lorenzen, my teammate, had come in after me, but they let him out seven seconds ahead of me. They kept my car jacked up so I couldn't move. I was furious.

But that was the guy Ford wanted to win. We were racing for the same team, but Lorenzen was their golden boy. When I finally got back out on the track, I chased him down and passed him. But I knew I couldn't shake him because he was the master of the draft.

I figured this is one of those deals where if you're not leading on the last lap, then you're not going to win, and there wasn't anything I could do about it. But then, with about three laps to go, we were coming down the back straightaway to lap Tiny Lund.

As we approached, Tiny motioned to me to go to the right while he went to the middle. Instead, I passed him by going way down on the inside, which startled Lorenzen for an instant, and I think he backed off. That's all I needed. Then it was all-out to the finish.

But there wasn't much of a celebration at the end.

I've always considered it to be a real compliment when people ask for an autograph. You get the feeling that they have followed your career, that they are interested in your life, and that they appreciate what you have done. And God, what bigger compliment is there than that?

I remember getting Rodger Ward's autograph and feeling that way. In fact, I think I only asked for three autographs in my life, the other two being Eddie Sachs and Pat O'Connor. Why Pat O'Connor? Because in 1957 Indy Cars ran at Monza and he had just come back. I wanted to ask him about that race.

And he was so gracious and accessible. I was really impressed by the way he took the time to talk with me. Unfortunately, the following year, I was witnessing my first Indianapolis 500 and he was killed in an accident in turn three. It turned out to be one of those twists of fate because the first big sprint car race I won happened to be the Pat O'Connor-Joe James Memorial in Salem, Indiana.

There are times, however, when the timing is all wrong and you can't stop what you're doing to sign autographs. At those moments, you wish you could at least explain so that everyone would understand. Other times, there might be a group of 30 and maybe you are only able to get to 15 or 20 of them. As a result, the others feel slighted. So it's not always a win-win situation.

But you really hope the ones you missed understand. I don't say this for the sake of public relations or anything else, but I sincerely believe the support of the fans, and the strength I have derived from them, has played a major part in keeping my career going. You need that little extra boost because this game can become so psychological.

I've said this many times; the obstacles are so overwhelming that it's easy to get down. So every ounce of strength, both physical and mental, becomes necessary. And that's something I have always been able to get from my fans.

In a sense, it's no different than a basketball team playing on its home floor. The reason the home team usually plays well has nothing to do with the court itself. The dimensions are the same, the basket is the same height. But it's the encouragement you feel when people are cheering you on. And it works.

Going to Monza the first time was indescribable because only a few years earlier it had been nothing more than a dream, a goal that seemed far beyond what my reasonable expectations should have been. I mean, that was the place I first started dreaming about racing. And then, when it happened, the feelings were so strong.

That's why the 1978 Italian Grand Prix represented so much more. Not only did I have a chance to win that race for the second year in a row, but I could win the World Championship at Monza as well.

I was on the pole with Jacques Villeneuve next to me in a Ferrari. But the start, and the whole day, for that matter, turned out to be traumatic. The problem at Monza is that the straightaway was nearly double the usual width because it served as the straightaway for the road surface and the high bank track. So at the start of the race everybody fanned out. But then, as you approached the first turn, they all had to come back together, which created a tunnel effect. And that's where they had a lot of accidents.

One of the worst happened that day right after the start. My teammate, Ronnie Petersen, got caught in the turn. Somebody came from the outside, squeezed him, and he had no place to go. It was an awful scene. Ronnie died as a result of the accident. I had known Ronnie since the early '70s, and he had probably the best car control of any driver I had ever known. He had been up to our place in the Poconos, and we had become such good buddies over the years.

Because of the accident, everyone was on edge. They delayed the race about 45 minutes and had a complete restart. In Grand Prix racing, within 10 seconds of the red light being displayed, the green light comes on. I always figured it took about seven seconds. But suddenly, with the red light still on, Villeneuve takes off. And I'm startled, so I start too, but I quickly stop just across the line. But he's gone and nearly into the chicane when the green light comes on.

I had a normal reaction because I was right next to him. Villeneuve never looked back. And even though they ended up penalizing us both 60 seconds, we ran as hard as you can run all day long. Then, two laps from the finish, I passed him for the lead and won the race.

Then I found out they had taken it all away. There we were up on the podium with the trophies and everything else, but the officials had given the race to Niki Lauda because of the penalty. But Lauda never came up to the podium. He felt like he didn't really win, so he wasn't going to stand for any of the accolades. He's quite a guy, and I have a lot of respect for him.

I really thought we would appeal, but after Ronnie died the next morning, we just let it drop. At that moment, all the energy just disappeared from my body. I remember thinking, 'How can I be worried about a freaking race?'

In the end, I didn't have to win that race to win the championship. At that point, Ronnie was the only driver that could have challenged me because he was the only one close enough.

So I lose one of my best buddies, they take the race away from me, and I win the World Championship. There wasn't much justice in that. It should have been the happiest day of my life, but there were these other elements.

And of all the tracks, it had to happen at Monza. I won the World Championship, but it came at a price, a helluva price.

Mr. Ferrari had absolute confidence. I remember when he was offering me a drive. He said, 'Mario, take a walk with me.' We looked into the shop where they made everything. He had engines, a foundry division, everything. So he said, 'Look at this. Every man in there is working for you.' He definitely had a way of putting things. And you know, it did get your attention.

The old man would be attacked by the media, and yet, he was always in complete control. At his annual press conference he'd go through his presentation and then say, 'OK, the floor is yours. Shoot, but aim correctly.' In other words, no bull.

And they knew. Enzo Ferrari had such command of the language, such absolute command, that you could see him destroy those guys. It was almost as if you could see them melt.

He wasn't a big man physically, but he was bigger than life. He had a way about him, a presence, and it was unmistakable.

And he was a great opportunist, a great manipulator. I mean, he built that entire company from scratch. Enzo had been a driver for Alfa Romeo, and although he wasn't a champion, he had been very prominent during that era. As the story went, Ferrari had been slighted in favor of a teammate. Enzo vowed that would never happen again. So he decided to build his own race cars.

He was really after me at the end of 1977, and I was in a position of strength because I had just won the Italian Grand Prix. So after Monza, I went to Maranello to hear what he had to say. At the time, I had shaken hands with Colin Chapman, promising to stay on for the 1978 season. But we didn't have a formal contract, and there were still some financial issues in dispute.

So I told the old man, 'Look, this may be a futile exercise for both of us because I basically have a deal which I may, in the end, have to honor.' He said, 'Well, that's why we have lawyers around.'

But we went through the process anyway. And with Italians, it's always delicate when the conversation turns to money. It comes down to the fact we have to agree on all points, so I asked him, 'What are you willing to pay?' And this is where he got me. He said, 'It's not for me to put a price on your talent. You have to tell me.' He threw it right back with a compliment besides. Now Dee Ann is sitting there, but she doesn't know what's going on because the conversation is in Italian. I couldn't even ask her for help. So I figured, well, Colin is paying me this much, so I'll go for double.

I shot Enzo the figure, and he didn't even flinch. He said, 'OK.'

I thought, well, let's see what Colin does. He immediately called Enzo, and the old man called me. He said, 'Look, this looks like more of a contract than I thought. Maybe we should let it go.'

And we did, but there were a lot of emotions because I really did want to drive for Ferrari. At the same time, we had started something with Lotus. There was a revolution going on with aerodynamics, and I was right in the middle of it. I knew I had to capitalize on that. Ultimately, I ended up driving my last Formula One race for Ferrari.

Another thing I'll never forget is the party he threw for all his drivers. The F40 car was named in honor of Ferrari's 40th year in business. Enzo invited all of the drivers that had ever driven for him to a party. The entire experience was beyond description.

I mean, the heroes of the 1950s were there. That was the only time I ever saw the man emotional with tears. And it was probably the only time it ever happened in public. As he looked around, he was telling us that we were the reason for Ferrari's success. That was the last time that I saw him alive.

The first time I saw anything about Indianapolis was in a movie that was playing in Italy, *To Please a Lady,* with Clark Gable and Barbara Stanwyck.

There was Clark Gable, a race driver, going through the midget races and dirt tracks before finally going to Indianapolis. Actually, the title of the movie in Italy was not the translation of *To Please a Lady.* In Italy, it was simply called *Indianapolis.* Now, when I saw *Indianapolis* on the marquee, I thought it didn't make sense. I remember it really catching my attention.

I was 14 and living in Lucca when the movie came out. It's amazing the kinds of things that stay in your mind. But I remember the cars

and everything else looking really foreign. Just the shape of the track alone was different because I didn't even know oval racing existed. I knew horses and dogs ran on ovals, but I didn't know there were cars running on ovals.

But Clark Gable was really debonair. In the old days, they used to say all the top drivers would walk the track. And there was this scene where he's walking in DuQuoin, Illinois, and he's touching the dirt to get a feel for the denseness of the clay. I tried to do some of that later on, but I never got much out of it.

So after the movie, I became interested. But what really got my attention was the first time that Bill Vukovich won. His name piqued my curiosity because it was Yugoslavian and we had just moved away from that area. Not only that, but he won at the average speed of over 200 kilometers an hour, which seemed incredible.

That's when I realized what Indianapolis was all about. And it was impressive, very impressive. But you couldn't buy a magazine in Italy and get that kind of information. The only races that were written about were those in which Ferrari was running. That's why Sebring was reported on in much greater depth than Indianapolis.

But all this came after my first real fascination with the sport. If I had been born in the United States, then Indianapolis probably would have represented my highest goal. For me, however, my most ambitious dreams were reserved for Formula One.

I always looked to the best and aspired to be just like them. But I never spoke about those goals out loud. As far-fetched as they were at that time, I thought I'd be ridiculed, so I always kept them to myself.

Just walking Indianapolis with my little grandson Marco in 1994 reminded me of one of those thoughts. The first time I did that at Indy, I was a spectator. My Uncle Louie and I walked the track together in 1958. And I remember looking back and saying to myself, 'Someday I'm going to win this thing.' I had to say that to myself. I mean, there I was, sitting the whole race in turn four, hoping to speak to one of the drivers or to at least get an autograph.

But my goals were always way beyond what I could see and completely beyond the scope of what should have been reasonable at the time.

I have always thought that there is more to motor racing, a lot more, than Indianapolis. There's no question—that race holds a premier spot in anyone's career. But I'll tell you what: Auto racing has a lot more to offer.

It's more than a bit unfair to judge a driver's career by his or her performance at Indianapolis. There have been a number of great champions that haven't won there, but they remain great champions, nonetheless. No one would say that Indy is any more a test of skill than any other track.

But the difference is the focus placed on that race. The attention is so intense that in some cases, results, or a lack of positive results, does seem to affect careers.

It's an old analogy, but I always use Dale Earnhardt and the Daytona 500. He won every event except that race. Does that make him a lesser driver? Hell no. He just hasn't been lucky.

So maybe you have to look beyond the immediate results and see how competitive drivers have been at Indianapolis. Michael is a good example. As much as he has controlled that race, you can't tell me that he doesn't know how to win the thing. I've always believed that if you can lead it, then you're capable of winning it.

When I look back at my life, I think, 'Thank God for the war,' because it opened up a whole new life we would not have been able to experience otherwise. I would not have been able to do what I have done had I stayed in Italy. I know that.

I'm not sure what life would have held, but I know my father had plans for our education. But would I have pursued what I really wanted? Would I have been free to chase my goals and live out my dreams? I don't know. Maybe I would have become a lawyer or a doctor. Those were my father's dreams for me, that's for sure.

So it was all a great blessing because none of this would have happened otherwise. I'm 110 percent certain of that. It's a perfect example of several negatives coming together to make a positive. And it's happened in my life, time and again.

Somehow, I have always had faith that there is a reason for everything that happens. People say I'm the eternal optimist. And I am, because what happened at the beginning of my life, the trauma and the effect it had on the family, helped to determine my future.

Perhaps we were victims in one respect, but it's almost as if everything was meant to be, as if those events were all a part of a master plan. That's the way I look at it. And I do believe in fate, because the more I analyze my life, the less able I am to point to anything else.

When you get down to individual moments such as Indianapolis and the way everything worked against me in 1969, I have to believe in fate. I was destined to win that race once. I was in control of winning it more often than that one time, but I was destined to win at least once. It was as if that day had been put into a vault. Fate gave me that.

I've been asked how I want to be remembered. Well, I think just as a guy that gave 110 percent, a man that really enjoyed his work. I love motor racing. It's been my life, and I've given it all I could.

That's all. Just a man who really enjoyed what he was doing.

Aldo and I were trying to be racers in Lucca when we were in our early teens. We were riding around a little parklike area which was near the train station.

This was our very first race car, a 1948 Hudson Hornet. Aldo and I had this picture taken with our partners right before we headed to the Nazareth track in 1959. We flipped a coin to see who would get the first ride. Aldo won the toss, and he ended up winning the race, too.

I'm not sure about the race track, but I know this picture was taken before the start of the race because I'm all clean. I can tell by the car that it was 1965.

Billy Foster was my best friend. What a guy. He was a tremendously talented Canadian driver who was killed in a race at Riverside in 1967.

I'm driving car No. 12 in the Hoosier Grand Prix at Indianapolis Raceway Park. This was my first Indy Car victory and the only race I won in 1965 on my way to the National Championship.

I was hit with a rock during a midget race and ended up with a shiner. But the worst incident with a rock was in the 1965 Hoosier 100. I was hit in the mouth on the second lap. When the race ended, the entire area around the injury was covered with dirt. I ended up with 19 stitches inside my mouth and another 11 on the outside.

The "M" on the bumper stood for the Mataka Brothers, who owned the car. This was taken in 1963 at an ARDC midget race in Thompson, Connecticut. I finished third that day.

Johnny Parsons spun in front of me and trapped me in the wall. That was at the Indianapolis 500 in 1983, my first year with Newman/Haas Racing.

That's me drinking my caffè latte in Montona, Italy, when I was about three.

This was one of the Viceroy cars, from either 1973 or 1974. I think I was pre-loading the roll bar. It's one of those things you can't explain to someone else, so I used to do it myself.

I narrowly avoided this crash at the start of the 1977 U.S. Grand Prix in Long Beach. I just made it underneath the accident. I ended up winning the race on the last lap.

One of the ways we keep fit is racing around our lake with our hydroplane, which Jeff is driving in this photo. We bought the boat from Molinari in Italy after it won the world championship in 1975.

I've had a lot of teammates; some of them have become very good friends. Other times, we each had our own agenda and we tended to go our separate ways. That's Nigel Mansell and me talking before the 1994 Indy 500.

This was taken in our trackside suite at Indianapolis in 1994. That's Jeff with his wife, Angelica, and my third grandchild, Miranda.

My friend, Dr. Larry Stephenson and I had this off-shore boat built especially for us in 1994. Mark McManus from Apache designed it to our specs with high-performance Mercury Marine engines and out-drives meticulously prepared under the supervision of Fred Kiekhaefer.

The Andretti family in 1969 with our dog, Todi, and cat, Samantha. The trophy over my left shoulder was given to me by the American Oil Company after I won Indy. They made it to match my exact height and weight.

One of my hobbies is flying my Quicksilver ultralight up at the lake. I especially enjoy the solitude and peacefulness in the evening when the winds are calm.

One of our friends had these signs made for us. It's not something we commissioned, but they have been up at the lake for about 15 years.

Thanks to Kenny Roberts, I was able to fulfill a lifelong dream by riding a Grand Prix bike. I really love motorcycles and that type of racing. I did five laps at Laguna Seca in 1992, and at the speed I was driving, I would have qualified 17th on the grid for the U.S. Grand Prix the year before.

In 1970, I flew over to Germany to get fitted for my new race car, a 1971 McNamara. The car was being built exclusively for our team owned by Andy Granatelli.

My mother, Rina, and my father, Gigi, which is short for Luigi, come up to the lake quite often. It's always nice having them there with us.

Aldo and I are sitting on the wall before a sprint car race in Oswego, New York, in 1967. It was the only time I raced against him and, as it turned out, I won.

Mark Vancil's Rare Air, Ltd. developed and produced *Rare Air: Michael on Michael*, Michael Jordan's pictorial autobiography, which was a #1 *New York Times* bestseller. Mark also developed and coordinated *I Can't Accept Not Trying*, Michael's most recent book. Previously, Mark worked 10 years as an award-winning writer/reporter for the *Chicago Sun-Times*, *Minneapolis Star-Tribune*, and *The National Sports Daily*. In addition to developing publishing projects, Mark provides creative direction and project coordination for a number of corporate and professional organizations.

McMillan Associates, a leading Chicago-based design firm, and designer of *Rare Air: Michael on Michael* and *I Can't Accept Not Trying*, has been in the business of creating award-winning visual communications and printed publications for 10 years. With an international roster of clients, McMillan Associates has a reputation for innovative approaches and solutions to communication design.

Walter Iooss Jr.'s photographs were used exclusively in *Rare Air: Michael on Michael*. Walter has been associated with *Sports Illustrated* for more than 25 years. His award-winning work has been exhibited in prestigious museums throughout the country.